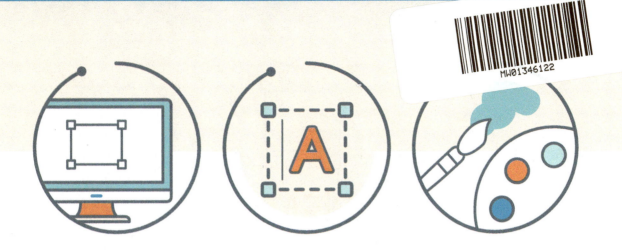

GRAPHIC DESIGN
Fundamentals

An Introduction & Workbook for Beginners

Including Project Resources, Inspiration Ideas, Project Planner, Adobe Illustrator Guide & More!

By
KRIS TAFT MILLER

DEDICATION

This book is dedicated to my three boys,
my two sons and my husband, who are
the reason for my everything.

Copyright © 2022 KT Design, LLC.
All rights reserved. No part of this book may be used or reproduced in any manner whatsoever or stored in any database or retrieval system without written permission except in the case of brief quotations used in critical articles and reviews. Requests for permissions should be addressed to:

KT Design, LLC
www.ktdesignacademy.com

ISBN: 978-1-7378206-3-5
Imprint: Independently published

TABLE *of* CONTENTS

Chapter One: Welcome & Introduction 4

Chapter Two: Common Terms of Graphic Design 6

Chapter Three: The Four Main Principles (CRAP) 9

Chapter Four: Composition & Balance 20

Chapter Five: Hierarchy & Visual Flow 27

Chapter Six: Optical Center & White Space 32

Chapter Seven: Let's Get Colorful! 35

Chapter Eight: Typeface or Font? 42

Chapter Nine: What Program to Use? 51

BONUS ONE: Design Inspiration Resources 54

BONUS TWO: Getting Started Workbook 61

BONUS THREE: Adobe Illustrator Guide 67

About the Author 90

Chapter One
WELCOME & INTRODUCTION

Welcome!

I am a big believer in jumping right in so let's get started. My name is Kris and in case you don't know anything about me here is a quick bio. I started my design career at Walt Disney Feature Animation where I was lucky enough to spend eight incredible years working on the animated films such as *Lilo & Stitch, Brother Bear, Meet the Robinsons, Chicken Little,* and even *Frozen* back when it was called *Snow Queen*, as well as many, many more. I left Disney because I met my husband who lived in North Carolina and decided it was the best time to start my own design agency. It was not the easiest thing to do and I learned a TON that first year. I actually have a degree in education and all of my graphic design training was on the job at Disney. I have been fortunate enough to establish a successful freelance career for the past 17 years and I am so looking forward to sharing what I have learned both at Disney and on my own.

The purpose of this book is to provide a beginner level education about graphic design. This includes common terms, basic design fundamentals, how to find inspiration, fonts (my favorite), and more! Most importantly, I want you to feel like you can jump right in and try your hand at designing!

I have created this guide while keeping four main goals in mind.

Number One:

I want you to feel comfortable in your design process – whatever that may be. Either you already have an idea of how you work best or you are still fine tuning that process. Let's clean it up and narrow it down until it is almost a science, and you will be able to work much more efficiently and successfully.

Number Two:

I want you to know the best practices about fundamental graphic design. This just means understanding the common terms that are used constantly in the graphic design world – what they mean, why they are important and how to ensure you are implementing them into your work. Keep them handy until you are super used to them.

Number Three:

I want you to truly understand how visual hierarchy works and all of the many ways to accomplish a successful layout. From composition, balance, and flow to space, color and fonts, we will dive into the details of each of these fundamentals to give you the foundation you need to truly create those design masterpieces you are capable of.

Number Four:

I want to introduce you to the tools you need to get you started quickly! From Canva to Adobe Illustrator, I am going to introduce you to several tools to help you in your design projects. People tell me all the time about how scary and overwhelming Illustrator or really any of the Adobe programs seems to be and they aren't wrong. You could spend your whole life learning new things to do in these programs. I learn new things ALL THE TIME. That should not stop you from STARTING. The bonus guide is designed to get you past that first hurdle and just START already! You can do this.

Make a Plan

Are you a planner? I am, by nature, NOT a planner. I am a jump in and start kind of person, which I believe is both good and bad, so what I do is force myself to slow down sometimes and make a plan. This can mean different things for different projects. I am going to show you some steps I have taken in the past to help me get organized and get started.

We are going to go over inspiration — where to find it, ways to sift through and organize it, and how best to utilize it.

But first we are going to quickly discuss copyright. It is real, and it is important and vital for designers to know and understand what copyright is and how to avoid copyright infringement. If you are drawing inspiration from a resource, then the most important thing to remember in regards to copyright infringement in my opinion is to be CERTAIN to create your own original artwork. If you are utilizing stock artwork, then you need to be comfortable reading the terms of use and how they relate to your project, including what your client intends to use the item for and so on. Logos, for example, should always be your own original work so they can always be trademarked if your client wants to do that.

Bottom line with copyright is: if you are in doubt...ASK. I have emailed resources many times asking for permission to use something or asking for clarification on their terms of use, often referred to as TOU. I know a very successful painter who often draws inspiration for her portraits from modeling images she finds online. She ALWAYS contacts the owner/model and researches how to gain proper permission to use the photograph as inspiration for her paintings.

Ok – enough about that – let's move on to the fun stuff!

I want to make it super clear that everyone will find different things that work for them, and I ask you to pay attention to your developing design sense and what works best for you. Take what works best and expand on that. The included workbook is intended to give you a jumping off point and options to consider.

Let's start with some common graphic design terms that you will hear over and over again.

Chapter Two
COMMON TERMS of GRAPHIC DESIGN

Bleed
Just that little bit of extra space...
Bleed is a printing term that refers to the edge of the sheet that will be trimmed off. In graphic design terms, the bleed is the artwork or background color that extends beyond the border into the bleed area, and must be taken into consideration to prevent any important artwork being trimmed off.

CMYK
For print...
CMYK, is the color mode which should be used when designing for print. The four colors the name stands for, Cyan, Magenta, Yellow and Key (Black), are the four colors most widely used in printing. These four colors can be combined to produce a majority of colors in print.

RGB
For the web...
Not to be confused with RBG (US Supreme Court Justice Ruth Bader Ginsberg), RGB simply stands for Red Green Blue. It is the color mode which should be used when designing for digital applications. The three colors combine to create any color in the visible spectrum.

Alignment
How things line up...
Alignment is the way that the different elements in a design are lined up, typically in relation to the page or other elements. In typography, alignment is how the text is positioned relative to a column, tab or page. Alignment is an important aspect of any design project.

Crop Marks
Where to cut...
Also known as trim marks, crop marks indicate to a printer where the paper should be trimmed. They're essential when designing for print and make it much easier to communicate what you want from specific printers.

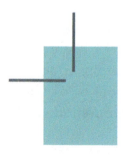

Graphic Design Fundamentals • An Introduction & Workbook for Beginners

GRAPHIC DESIGN
Common Terms

Hierarchy
Where to look...
One of the five basic principles of typography design, hierarchy creates organization and direction in a design. It essentially is the order of items that your eye goes to when viewing a design. You have definitely seen hierarchy in action in pretty much anything you have read. It makes text more understandable and easier to read.

Pixel
They make up everything...
A mix of the words 'picture' and 'element', a pixel is the smallest basic unit of programmable color on a computer and all digital images are made up of a large number of individual pixels. Think of them as tiny squares that make up an image.

PPI & DPI
How they measure up...
These are two measurements used to measure the resolution of an image. PPI stands for pixels per inch and DPI stands for dots per inch. They refer to the amount of pixels or dots that can be placed in a line across one linear inch. PPI is used to describe the resolution of a digital image and DPI is used to describe the amount of ink dots per inch in a printed image.

Industry Standard:
Print: 300 DPI
Web: 72 PPI

Raster
It is what it is...
A raster is an image made up of a certain number of pixels. Each pixel has its own color, hue, saturation and transparency which helps to make up the image as a whole. Unlike vectors, raster images will lose quality and become blurry as they are resized, due to them being made up of pixels.

Vector
The sky is the limit...
A vector is a graphic image that is made with mathematical equations—they're defined in terms of 2D points connected by lines and curves to form shapes. Basically this means that vectors can be resized or scaled to any size without losing quality or getting blurry. They are the most useful and versatile graphic image.

Graphic Design Fundamentals • An Introduction & Workbook for Beginners

GRAPHIC DESIGN
Common Terms

White or Negative Space
Let it breathe...
White space, or padding, actually does not need to be white. It is the space, which can be any color, pattern or texture, between different elements in a design that is essential in creating a successful layout. Think of white space as giving a design visual breathing room, like some sort of design meditation.

File Formats:

AI
Adobe Illustrator
This is the native Illustrator file format, and I always save my source files as this so that I always have them for future edits, etc.

PDF
Portable Document Format
This format is used when you need to save files that cannot be modified, but still need to be easily shared and printed. Today almost everyone has a version of Adobe Reader or another program on their computer that can read a PDF file. However, you can save a PDF in Illustrator that others can see who might not own Illustrator but it can be saved **preserving the Illustrator editing capabilities** so that it can still be edited as a vector file.

EPS
Encapsulated PostScript
An EPS file is helpful because virtually all page layout, word-processing, and graphic applications accept imported or placed EPS files. The EPS format preserves many of the graphic elements you can create with Adobe Illustrator, which means that EPS files can be reopened and edited as Illustrator files.

SVG
Scalable Vector Graphics
SVG files or are ideal for saving, as the name suggests, vector images (geometrically composed images based on points, lines, curves, polygons etc.) Advantages for this format are: Potentially smaller file sizes than their rasterized counterparts (jpg, png, gif).

Chapter Three
THE FOUR MAIN PRINCIPLES
C.R.A.P.

Whenever I hear "don't judge a book by its cover," I think to myself that this is essentially my entire job. When it comes to graphic design, everyone definitely does judge the book by it's cover. The purpose of a great design is communication. Getting your point across with a design is the ultimate goal so how well does your design communicate what you are trying to say is something you should always be asking yourself.

When you find yourself noticing an ad, a label, or packaging, ask yourself what it communicates to you. Do you remember a time you chose an item based on what the design looked like? It happens all the time, probably most of the time, without us ever thinking about it. With great graphic design comes great power!

This power can be simplified into four main principles which are the keys to unlocking your design expertise. It is as easy to remember as the simple acronym of CRAP. Yep. CRAP. Contrast, repetition, alignment and proximity. These four basic ideas will provide the understanding you need to discern graphic design "crap" from graphic design masterpieces.

Contrast

First up is the principle of contrast, a super powerful design concept that allows the designer to direct the viewer's attention by creating the hierarchy of the design. Simply put, where do you want the viewer to look first, second and so on. Using such elements as size, shape, color, direction, and so on, you can customize your designs to communicate your message effectively.

An important thing to remember with contrast is that the intended differences must be obvious. Small differences will not convey that one element is more important than another. By that same token, using too much contrast can create a chaotic design that confuses the viewer. As with many things in life, a good rule is everything in moderation.

Here are some examples of designs and how contrast is used to create hierarchy.

The size of the headline is intended to draw the eye, followed by the date and then the pricing information.

Graphic Design Fundamentals • An Introduction & Workbook for Beginners

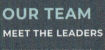

Contrast can be created by differentiating a section with a different background color.

Here the use of size creates a nice visual contrast for the chapter header in an appealing, clean, and clear manner.

Contrast can also be created by how you use your space. The placement of your design's elements alters the appearance immensely.

Repetition

The principle of repetition is basically self explanatory. Repeat, repeat, repeat! Establish a brand, look, style, and feel to your design and REPEAT those elements throughout your design to create unity and cohesion.

The purpose of contrast is to create differences leading to hierarchy, while the purpose of repetition is to bring everything together. Repetitive elements can include a color scheme, similar shapes, patterns, lines, fonts, borders and so on.

Repetition is the most important when the project has multiple pages, such as a book, brochure, or presentation. Creating a cohesive look before beginning projects like these will help support this design principle.

This does not mean that a poster, invitation or other single page design does not need repetition to be successful. Using repetition in this case will help a viewer instantly group items that are related together while differentiating others, such as "action items" like buttons and headlines.

Here is an example of repeating the same color scheme, font choice, and element style throughout multiple pages of a design, creating cohesion with a branded look.

Here is the same design with three different fonts, three different line styles, and each page with a different color scheme, creating a chaotic visual that does not appear to go together in the same design concept.

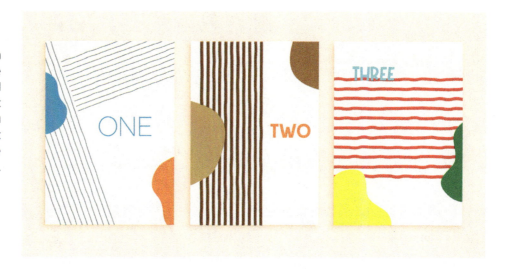

Graphic Design Fundamentals • An Introduction & Workbook for Beginners

Alignment

The principle of alignment is seemingly straightforward, but must be used correctly to keep your design looking professional and polished. The alignment principle's purpose is that nothing in your design should look like it is floating in outer space. Every element should be anchored to something else.

Imagine invisible lines connecting everything in your design. Luckily, there are these awesome align tools in every design program these days making this step a breeze.

There are four main alignment options. Perhaps the most common would be using the left side or edge of a word or object. Alternatively, you can use the right side or edge of something to align to. Another would be using the center of an element, and lastly would be justified or "forced" alignment. Let's discuss each one in a little more detail in relation to graphic design specifically.

Compare these two very similar business card designs that are the same in color scheme, font, and style but with very different alignment. Alignment creates organization and prevents chaos.

Left Alignment

This is most often used with larger bodies of text, such as books, but is also largely used for paragraphs on advertisements, brochures, and so on. Left alignment is considered the most legible for readability. It is important to note that if you have a subheader that is connected to a left aligned paragraph, you should align that subheader to the left as well (as seen below).

That is an example of left alignment where the left edges are aligned from the very top to the bottom of the page. The second example above shows how it looks if you try to center the headers when the text is left aligned. The only time that centering a headline with left aligned body text is appropriate would be when there is a good amount of space between the headline and the body text (as seen to the right).

Graphic Design Fundamentals • An Introduction & Workbook for Beginners

Right Alignment

This may be the least used alignment option. However, it can create visual interest especially if the intention is for an unconventional design. Right alignment works for shorter text blocks but should not be used for larger bodies of text. It is important to note that some languages are read right to left (e.g. Japanese, Korean, Arabic), and should use right alignment as you would use left alignment for English and other left to right languages.

Here is an example of using right alignment to create a visually interesting layout for an ad.

Right alignment can be useful in items such as business cards, posters, or other items where you want to use it as a design element, and there is not a lot of text. Here is an example of using right alignment versus center alignment in a report cover design to achieve a more unique look.

Center Alignment

I would say this is the most overused alignment option by beginning designers. The instinct can be to center everything. This is often not the best option and can make things harder to read. Headlines are often your best bet for center alignment as well as designs where little text is actually used, such as a web banner or advertisement. Experiment with different alignments in your designs before centering everything.

Here is an example of a bright, simple, effective advertisement that uses center alignment effectively.

Invitations are another example of a project that can effectively utilize center alignment for all of the text.

Justified Alignment

This is also called forced alignment as it basically forces the text to align to both the right and left margins. This is most often used in books, magazines, newspapers, and other publications that utilize columns. Here is an example of a justified version of book layout versus a left aligned option.

Graphic Design Fundamentals • *An Introduction & Workbook for Beginners*

Justified alignment can create a more formal appearance but can create spacing issues if the column of text is too narrow and the words are too long (as shown below on the left). Make sure you have the adequate width to accommodate the size of the text you want to use justified alignment with (as shown below).

Header

Subheader
Lorem ipsum dolor sit amet, consectetuer adipiscing elit, sed diam nonummy

Header

Subheader
Lorem ipsum dolor sit amet, consectetuer adipiscing elit, sed diam nonummy nibh euismod tincidunt ut laoreet dolore magna aliquam erat volutpat. Ut wisi enim ad minim veniam.Lorem ipsum dolor sit amet, consectetuer adipiscing elit, sed diam nonummy nibh euismod tincidunt ut laoreet dolore magna aliquam

Alignment can be almost imperceptible to your viewer, but if something is just a little 'off' they will notice it and it won't look right. Utilize those alignment tools and experiment with different options.

Proximity
The intention of your design should be to communicate the message to your viewer as quickly as possible. By creating a clean and organized design, you can make it so the the viewer should be able to easily follow the flow of the message and never have to struggle to understand the intent. This brings us to proximity which is the fourth main principle whose main purpose is to organize.

Going back to the idea of hierarchy again, always be thinking about where you want the viewer to look first, second, third, and so on. Organize and group your elements in your design in the way that makes the most sense to the viewer. Don't make them search for information.

By using such components as size, shape, color, and so on, you can group your elements in a way to differentiate or relate when needed. The more organized your design, the more quickly your viewer can process each element or group of elements and understand the message, which is the entire point!

Here is a very basic example of grouping by differentiating subheaders in a list.

Option One

Chicken

Beef

Option Two

Potatoes

Salad

Option Three

Chocolate Cake

Ice Cream

Option One

Chicken

Beef

Option Two

Potatoes

Salad

Option Three

Chocolate Cake

Ice Cream

Using that same idea with graphical elements, you can create groups to organize your design and allow the viewers eye to process them more effectively. Here is an example of an organized group and an unorganized group of the same graphic elements.

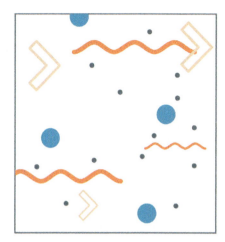

The most extreme proximity relationship you can establish is to layer your elements. Here is an example of a simple sales badge with and without using layering proximity.

Proximity can also be created using borders, boxes, banners, lines, shapes, etc. Here is a basic ad that shows how keeping all the important information grouped helps the viewer easily absorb the messaging versus the same ad with the information scattered.

Graphic Design Fundamentals • An Introduction & Workbook for Beginners

Using these four main principles, you are well on your way to knowing how to lay out an effective, visually appealing design that will communicate your messages in a cohesive and comprehensive way.

Let's bring them all together and redesign this advertisement using those four principles as a guide.

First thing we can improve is the **contrast**. We can increase the size of the headline to draw attention and utilize different colors to break up the text.

By changing some of the border's widths and colors we can start to bring **repetition** into this design to create cohesion. We can also add an element that we can repeat throughout to bring visual interest as well as unifying the design.

We can also easily improve the **alignment**. Let's go with a left alignment option and bring everything together visually.

Finally, we can improve the **proximity** of related elements to increase the speed at which the viewer can grasp the message and ultimately act on the directed message, which is to get them to click on the button to learn more.

What an improvement! The C.R.A.P. principles are laid out for you on the next page. You can always make a copy of that page and post it near your work space so you can reference it as you get started with your own designs.

PRINCIPLES *of* DESIGN

CONTRAST

One of the most useful design principles, contrast, is used to differentiate elements of a design, creating hierarchy, and drawing the viewer's eye in a natural flow to the aspects of a design in order of importance.

This can be accomplished in many ways, such as size, color, shape, space, font, and so on.

SIZE

SHAPE

COLOR

FONT

REPETITION

Repetition is part of creating a cohesive brand. Create a style for the elements of your design, whether that be the font, color scheme, style etc. and repeat it throughout your design to establish a pattern of consistency.

Repeat, repeat, repeat.

ALIGNMENT

Basically, nothing should be floating around in space in a design. Each element should be anchored to something else and the simplest way to do that is using alignment. By aligning one element to another you are creating a cohesive, clear, connected visual.

PROXIMITY

The simplest way to put this is to keep things that are related close to each other. This is vital for the organization of your design to allow it to communicate effectively and isn't that the whole point?

Create understanding by keeping it clean and clear.

Graphic Design Fundamentals • An Introduction & Workbook for Beginners

Chapter Four
COMPOSITION & BALANCE

Composition

You hear a lot about cohesion in design. The composition of your design is basically whether you have achieved cohesion. A successful composition is when all of your graphic design elements have come together to cohesively communicate the message you intended. So, the final visual should not only "be pretty", but also effective in order to be considered a successful composition.

How do we achieve a successful composition?

The first step is implementing the C.R.A.P principles that we just covered. Another step would be to strive for visual **balance**.

Visual balance is all about how your design attracts the viewers eye. If all of the design elements are arranged so that no one aspect overpowers the whole visual then balance has successfully been achieved.

Sounds simple enough, right? Unfortunately, it is a little more complicated than that. With too much balance, comes boredom. With too little, comes chaos. Achieving that **perfect** balance is what you are after.

There are **FOUR** main types of compositional balance that you can aim for. Symmetrical, asymmetrical, radial and crystallographic.

Symmetrical Balance

This seems like the most obvious idea of balance, right? Although there are three other types of visual balance, this one influences all of them. Symmetrical balance is achieved by giving equal weight to elements in your design on either side of a center point in the composition. The center can be horizontal, vertical, or diagonal. This results in a mirrored or repetitive visual effect that appears balanced. Our natural instincts tend to prefer symmetry, so this is a very useful balance option.

Faces are often perceived as more traditionally beautiful if they are symmetrical. Butterflies are another good example of symmetrical beauty in nature.

This type of balance works particularly well for wider layouts where the designer can repeat elements across, bringing cohesion. In symmetrical designs, the eye is naturally drawn to the center point. Using this focal point for the most important element of your design is key, whether it is your headline or a call-to-action item.

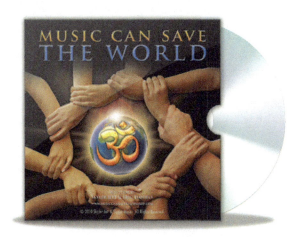

It is possible for this balance style to become too repetitive and therefore boring. Utilizing a different element somewhere in the design keeps the viewer's eye engaged and active.

Asymmetrical Balance

Compared to symmetrical balance, asymmetrical balance tends to create more visually appealing compositions because they are more dynamic and visually engaging. Asymmetrical balance occurs when the elements of a design are different but are still being weighed and laid out in a visually balanced manner. This is not as easily done as symmetrical balance and can require some trial and error.

The easiest way to start out with asymmetrical balance in a design is to draw a line through the center of the layout in any direction and then place your elements in an unequal pattern.

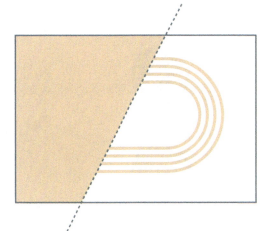

The idea of asymmetrical balance is to keep the viewer's eye engaged because they have to pay more attention to follow the design, but still have balance to be successful in communicating the message. Using different sizes, colors, shapes, contrasts, and so on can create asymmetrical balance with practice.

Graphic Design Fundamentals • An Introduction & Workbook for Beginners

Below are some things to keep in mind when you are creating asymmetrical balance.

A S Y M M E T R I C A L

MORE ATTENTION	LESS ATTENTION
DARK	LIGHT
LARGE	SMALL
TEXTURE	FLAT
WARM COLORS	COOL COLORS
ONE ITEM	ONE OF MANY

Radial Balance

This is the most soothing balance option. It is typically created by using a radial elements, such as water ripples, rays of sunlights, or any spiral feature to draw the eye to a center focal point. Radial balance often occurs in natural elements such as seashells, trees, flowers, etc.

Flyers or posters with little content often use radial balance to draw the viewer's eye to the main message quickly.

You can use the two opposing ideas of symmetry and asymmetry together to create a powerful design. Balance asymmetrical forms symmetrically or vice versa. By utilizing both of these balance principles you create contrast which, as we know, is one of the keys to an effective composition.

Graphic Design Fundamentals • An Introduction & Workbook for Beginners

Crystallographic Balance

This one is a mouthful, so another way to say it is "mosaic" balance. This type of balance is best summarized with the idea of organized chaos. By giving several design elements equal weight, the composition almost tricks the viewer into thinking that the design is balanced, even with a large amount of randomness going on.

Design layouts with too little going on cannot achieve this type of balance as it allows the viewer's eye to linger on individual items instead of creating a cohesive look. You can use different or similar elements to repeat and create a mosaic effect. Utilizing different sizes, shapes, and colors, you can create an appealing and natural layout. In this balance option, using different sizes effectively will actually end up feeling more natural and appealing to the viewer. Using complementary color schemes can also bring the mosaic design together in a more balanced appearance.

Visual balance is one of those design aspects that is often overlooked as it usually comes down to a feeling. You cannot always describe why it is or isn't there, but you know when it is and isn't there.

The Golden Ratio

Have you heard of the all important Golden Ratio? It dates back to ancient Greece but is still super relevant in design today. It refers to the Greek letter phi and relates to the number 1.61803398875.... Don't worry, you don't have to remember that number. In mathematical terms, it is an irrational number – an endless series of digits that don't repeat and can't be expressed as a fraction. If you are like me, then a little more visualization always helps – see below.

THE GOLDEN RATIO

| A | B |

$$\frac{A}{B} = \frac{A+B}{A} = 1.61...$$

What it boils down to is this. If you apply the rule of 1 to 1.61 in a composition then it will look both balanced and natural. The Golden Ratio is considered to be represented in such historical designs as the pyramids, Salvador Dali's work, Michelangelo's masterpieces, and even Stonehenge. If you look around today, you will find it in many of the most popular logos, brands, and photographs. Here is the Golden Ratio as a visual representation you probably recognize.

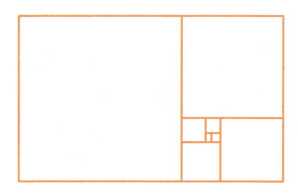

What this means is that math is often the reason that an object or visual has a striking appearance or natural beauty. The human body is also a representation of the Golden Ratio with its symmetry and proportions.

The Golden Spiral is important to note as well as this is closely related to the Golden Ratio. This is the spiral that is seen all over nature – seashells, flowers, seeds, bees, starfish, dolphins, the list goes on and on.

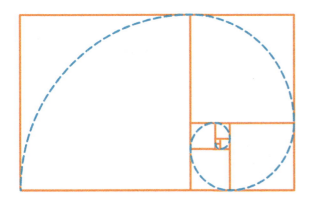

As you begin to visualize how these number sequences come together to create beauty in nature and design, you will start to see it everywhere. So how can we use it in design effectively?

The Golden Ratio can be used to guide how design elements are placed, whether it be a magazine layout, logo design or web page. For instance, in a column layout on a website, you could design a layout with a larger content column on the left and a sidebar column on the right. Using the Golden Ratio calculator, you can get exact proportions, but getting close to the 1 to 1.61 ratio is the goal. The reason you see this all over the internet is that it is highly effective.

The Golden Ratio is key to developing effective hierarchy of a design and pulling the viewer's eye on your intended path. It can help you make decisions about where to place your elements as well as the ideal amount of white space. Once you master the Golden Ratio rules you will find it allows you to more quickly optimize your work.

Now, I happen to like math, but I am also a very visual person and do not really want to focus on math when I am working on a design. So here is a way to use the Golden Ratio visually.

Start with a rectangle split into the Golden Ratio and then overlayed with a Golden Spiral to break it down into six parts (as shown on the left). Now draw a perfect circle in each one of those parts. These are called Golden Circles.

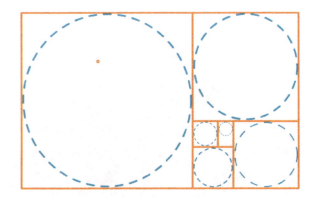

From here you can take those Golden Circles and rearrange them, overlap them, intersect them, and so on to create a design using the Golden Ratio ideals.

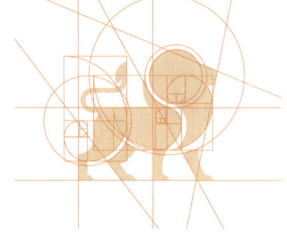

Once you understand the Golden Ratio, you don't need to worry so much about the mundane idea of overlaying all those circles or measuring your 1 to 1.61 ratio. You will start to find that you automatically incorporate the ideals of it without even realizing it. While this ancient visual idea may not seem like something you need to know, it can be an important and powerful principle to help you create engaging designs that your customers or clients can't help but be drawn to.

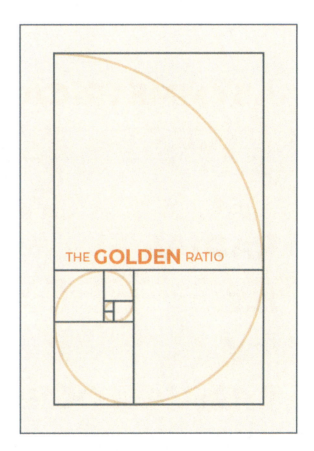

Graphic Design Fundamentals • An Introduction & Workbook for Beginners

TYPES *of* BALANCE

SYMMETRICAL

Symmetrical balance is created by giving equal weight to design elements across the horizontal, vertical, or diagonal center of a composition.

ASYMMETRICAL

Asymmetrical balance happens when the design elements on a layout are different in color, size, shape, etc., but by being equally weighted they still feel balanced.

RADIAL

Often occurring in nature, radial balance has a soothing and calming quality naturally drawing the eye towards a central focal point.

CRYSTALLOGRAPHIC

Crystallographic (or mosaic) balance gives equal weight to a large number of elements resulting in a type of balanced chaos that combines to create unified composition.

THE GOLDEN RATIO

The Golden Ratio is equal to 1 to 1.61 and can be used to create a visually appealing design that appears both natural and balanced. It is the foundation of numerous architecture, design and art masterpieces.

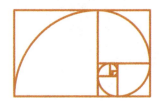

Chapter Five
HIERARCHY & VISUAL FLOW

Establishing Hierarchy

A huge part of effective graphic design is leading the viewer's eye in the order you intended. What is the specific information that you want them to see first, second, and so on? Where are your call-to-action items, and how can you direct their eye to them? You have the ability to create a visual flow to lead your viewer through your message effectively by purposefully arranging your design elements in such a way as to control the order in which the elements are perceived.

Typically, you want the viewer to look at headlines, titles, names, dates, and whatever the most important part of your message happens to be first. The secondary details like location, contact information and fine print should all be read after your main message.

There are so many ways to establish this idea of hierarchy in design – here are a few to think about as you create your own designs.

Color & Contrast

Color is such an important part of graphic design. Learning to use color with intention will help you manipulate the focus of your designs. The goal is to get noticed which is accomplished using contrast. Remember, warm and bright colors tend to stand out more than cool colors, especially against a darker background. Red, for instance, is often used to attract attention, like stop signs and message alerts. Different colors evoke different moods and emotional reactions. The trick is to blend your color choice with your design to convey the intended mood while being the most legible possible.

Contrast is something we have already covered, although it bears repeating as it is always important. This principle ultimately keeps your design from being boring! Achieving visual contrast with color, font, size and so on helps to build a successful hierarchy. Mastering the art of contrast will help bring your designs to a whole new level.

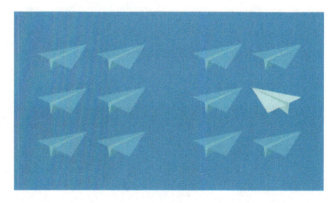
BEFORE   AFTER

Leading Lines

Using an arrow or object with a point is an especially easy way to direct a viewer's eye and impact the hierarchy of your design. As you can see, it quite literally shows the viewer where to look in this design.

BEFORE AFTER

Size Matters!

As expected, elements of your design that are larger in scale will get noticed first. This is why headings and titles are usually the largest text in a layout as well as images, illustrations and any other elements that the designer wants to use to dominate the top of the hierarchy chain. It is not only the size of an element but also the size in relation to the other elements. This is where proximity comes into play again as well. How large something is and how large it is compared to what is nearby matters. When using size or scale to focus your hierarchy, don't be afraid to go for it and make sure there is no confusion about what is the largest and most important element.

BEFORE AFTER

Fonts, Fonts, Fonts

You can get lost in fonts if you aren't careful. I know I have. Choosing a font can be a big decision, especially if the headline or title is going to be your main focal point. The choice of font should complement the feel of your overall design, whether it is modern, rustic, antique, playful, etc. A common mistake that new designers make is choosing a font that lacks readability. Picking a font that is fun but not legible is a mistake. Using a script font in all caps is a personal pet peeve of mine, and I cannot, for the life of me, think of an instance where that would ever make sense. Don't do it. Please.

When using more than one font, it is crucial to make sure they pair well together. Some questions to consider would be: do they complement each other? Are they too similar or too different? Do they contrast nicely or do they compete with each other? A general rule is not to go over three different fonts in one design. I typically stick to two unless something really calls for a third. When you choose to stick to one font then it can be fun to play with the weight and size of that font for different elements in your design.

BEFORE AFTER

Alignment

Alignment should be a familiar idea and one that doesn't need much explanation. The principle of alignment is especially important in a design that contains a lot of text elements. Keeping things clean and organized can be key to get all of your information across effectively. Centering headlines, using subheaders, and left aligning body text can help your viewer read things in order without difficulty. Alignment can also refer to lining up the graphical elements, illustrations, lines, images, etc. with each other or with the text. Using the handy alignment tools in many design programs makes this a breeze!

Proximity

This should also be familiar from the C.R.A.P. foundation principles we discussed. It is quite simply putting related elements of your design together to allow the viewer's eye to absorb related content quickly. By that same token, unrelated items should be spaced apart. Following the proximity principle helps create organization and flow in your designs.

Rule of Thirds

This is most easily illustrated by overlaying a grid on top of your image, illustration, or layout which will divide it into thirds, giving you nine equal boxes. If you look at successful paintings, photographs, and layouts, you will notice that rarely is the main subject centered. The focal points of the grid are where the lines cross. This gives you four focal points to utilize in your design to make the most impact. Positioning the call-to-actions or most important information in these areas is one key to successfully conveying your message.

Negative or White Space

Negative space, also called white space, is not necessarily white and can actually be one of the hardest concepts for new designers to master. The desire to fill the space can be tempting. Try to resist it! White space refers to the literal space around a design element, whether it be the title, images, or content. It is just as important as the design elements. I like to think of it as giving things room to breathe. White space helps establish an effective design hierarchy and keeps things from becoming unorganized and difficult to read.

Perspective

This idea is as easy as remembering that you can show something from a different angle to add visual interest to your designs. Simply put, remember to look at all perspectives.

seen in multiple page layouts such as books, magazine, websites, etc. Repeating elements can be things such as colors, fonts, lines, shapes, sizes, textures, patterns, and so on.

Rule of Odds

The Rule of Odds is just like it sounds: an odd number of items are often more visually appealing in a layout design, the most common choice being three items. The two items on the sides of the dominant item serve to create a simple, natural balance. You will see this often in logo designs with elements serving to offset a center item.

Eye-line

Finally, this is a great way to establish hierarchy in a design when you have an image or illustration that has a character, whether human, animal, or cartoon. Using the character's eye-line to direct the viewer to what you want them to see is a super effective way to establish hierarchy. As a general rule, the eye-line of a character should at the very least be directed towards the content of the page and not off the page.

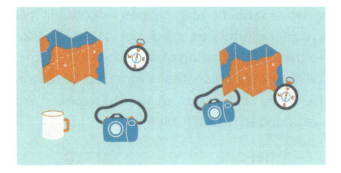

Repetition

Another one of our familiar fundamental principles to revisit when establishing hierarchy is repetition. So, to repeat, the principle of repetition involves utilizing the same or similar styled elements throughout a design to create cohesion. This is most often

Graphic Design Fundamentals • An Introduction & Workbook for Beginners

12 Hierarchy Principles

COLOR & CONTRAST

LEADING LINES

FONTS

RULE OF THIRDS

PROXIMITY

PERSPECTIVE

NEGATIVE SPACE

EYE-LINE

ALIGNMENT

RULE OF ODDS

REPETITION

SIZE & SCALE

Graphic Design Fundamentals • An Introduction & Workbook for Beginners

Chapter Six
OPTICAL CENTER & WHITE SPACE

Optical Center

The actual mathematical center point of a design is not actually where your eye perceives the center to be. This point where your eye perceives center is called the optical center. Typically, the optical center is just a little bit above the mathematical center, which is important to keep in mind in design. Utilizing the optical center can help draw the focus to the specific information that is most important. Optical center can be accentuated using many of the principles we have been discussing such as contrast, color, size, etc.

While the mathematical center is 50% down from the top of a page or design, the optical center falls around 46% down from the top of the page. So, how do you apply this concept into your designs?

CENTERED   **ADJUSTED**

There are two optical centers — a vertical and a horizontal. Both of them can play tricks on you. Just like the vertical center, the horizontal center can make something look off centered to the viewer's eye even when it is exactly aligned to the center. This phenomenon especially happens when the element is an irregular shape, as seen below. The first one shows the item mathematically perfectly horizontally centered but to our eye it looks too far to the right. The second one shows it manually maneuvered to the left just a bit giving the optical illusion of being centered.

50%   **46%**

If you mathematically center text or a graphic in your design, you'll notice that your content will seem a bit low. This is easily solved! Just adjust it manually so that it is slightly higher. Notice in this example how that slight adjustment makes a big visual difference?

CENTERED   **ADJUSTED**

Graphic Design Fundamentals • An Introduction & Workbook for Beginners

White Space

Since this concept is one that I believe newer designers sometimes struggle with, I wanted to delve a little deeper into how you can learn to manipulate your white space to work for you effectively.

Every blank canvas is nothing but white space to start with. This white space is undefined and not intentional. Once you start adding your elements the spaces that are formed are intentional and should be thoughtfully considered. As I mentioned before, white space does not mean in any way that it has to be white. It can be any color. It is all about giving your design breathing room and allowing the information to be organized in a clean, easily interpreted manner.

So, what are some best practices to create white or negative space in your designs? First of all, don't fear it. Don't feel like you have to fill every available inch of a design with content. Including white space truly is essential for creating a successful design.

One quick way to check your white space is to check your margins. Did you leave room around the edge of your layout between content and the border? As you can see here this is the visual impact that different margin sizes can have on a design.

Another easy way to achieve white space is to reduce the size of your elements. More often than not your design elements are larger than they need to be. Whether it is reducing a font point size or shrinking an illustration or icon, experiment to see if reducing the size actually gives your design the room to breathe that it ultimately needed.

BEFORE

AFTER

NO MARGINS

MARGINS

Graphic Design Fundamentals • An Introduction & Workbook for Beginners

Yet another way is to see if there is anything you can trim. Evaluate each element and its necessity to the overall message of the design. Is it helping to achieve what you are trying to convey effectively? If you aren't sure, try deleting it and see if you miss it. You might be surprised how the basic idea of simplifying — less is more — can be what your design needed all along.

BEFORE

AFTER

Using negative space in a logo design can be extremely effective and visually interesting. It can also be much harder than it sounds and can actually take the most skilled use of white or negative space to achieve. This can be especially true of those clever logos that have hidden elements incorporated into their white space, possibly the most famous logo that uses white space effectively is the arrow in the FedEx logo.

Another example would be the Goodwill logo where you can see there is half of a smiling face in the shape of a "g". Amazon is another great example. Their smiling arrow goes from the letter "a" to the letter "z", expressing that there is virtually nothing you can't find on Amazon because they offer everything from "A to Z". Maybe one of my favorite logos with negative space is the Apple logo. I have read that there is some debate over whether the bite out of the apple was to represent a computer "byte" or whether it was simply to differentiate it from a cherry. Once you start to examine logos you will never look at a logo design quite the same way again.

By harnessing the power of the "nothing" in your designs, you can make that white space work for you in creating hierarchy, flow, and visual appeal.

Chapter Seven
LET'S GET COLORFUL!

Choosing Colors

Color is one of the most powerful design tools, and therefore it is important to gain an understanding of all of the different impacts it can have. It can set the emotion and mood of your design and repel or attract the viewer's attention. The good thing is you don't have to reinvent the wheel, pun intended, as the color wheel already exists. By learning to follow the already established guidelines in the color wheel world, you can easily select color schemes for your projects.

Let's start at the very beginning. The primary colors of red, yellow, and blue. You can create any color by mixing these three colors together in different ratios.

If you equally mix two primary colors you get a secondary color, as show below.

From there if you mix any of the colors with the color next to them you will get tertiary colors, filling in your color wheel. These colors are called hues and are the foundation for all other color variations.

Tints

By adding white or black to a color you get different tints, shades, and tones. If you use white to lighten the color hues, you create tints or pastels. Adding white to a color lightens it, desaturates it, and makes it less visually intense. These colors tend to evoke a calm, quiet mood, such as a spa or therapist.

Graphic Design Fundamentals • An Introduction & Workbook for Beginners

Shades

To push your color in the opposite direction you can add black, which would make a hue darker and create what is called a shade of that color. The darker shades are best to use minimally in most designs so as not to weigh it down too much.

SHADES

Tones

Tints and shades can often need some toning down to make more user friendly and this is where tones come in. A tone is created by adding both black and white, or gray, to a color. For whatever reason, tones are more visually appealing to the viewer's eye. Most colors you see in the marketing world have been toned down to some degree.

TONES

Creating Tints, Shades and Tones

Whatever design tool you are using should have the ability to create your own color combinations and variants. I typically use Adobe Illustrator, which has a color picker like the one to the right, and I can mix up my own tints, shades, and tones by adjusting the levels of white, black, and gray. I can also save my color creations to easily bring up a palette I have made to use again.

Cool and Warm Colors

Now that we have a full color wheel we can split it down the middle into warm and cool colors. They are basically just like what they sound like. Cool colors evoke feelings of ice, winter, and chill, while warm colors create a feeling of heat, light, and intensity. What happens when cool colors meet warm colors? They create a hybrid color that can be warm or cool. Think of all of the different varieties of the hybrid color of purple for example. There is the lavender kind of color, which has more blue in it and is therefore a cooler color, and then there is the more pinkish purples, which have more red in them and are therefore considered warm.

WARM

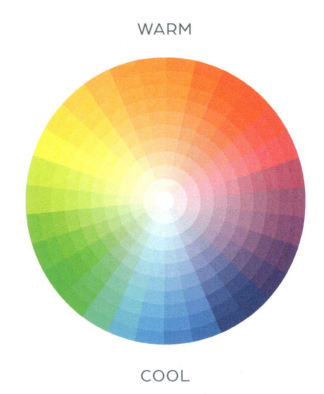

COOL

Complementary Colors

Colors that are opposite each other on the color wheel are called complementary colors. Choosing complementary colors will give you one cool and one warm color. Using complementary colors in a design creates contrast and can be used to emphasize design elements. Using complementary colors in a design should be done with restraint, so as not to allow each color to overwhelm the other and ultimately create visual chaos.

COMPLEMENTARY

Split Complementary Colors

This kind of color scheme is comprised of three hues. These color combinations are found by drawing a Y shape on a color wheel using one hue as the bottom and then the two adjacent colors to that hue's complementary color. This combination can achieve contrast without as much adversity as complementary color schemes and is often the easiest to use successfully.

SPLIT COMPLEMENTARY

Square Complementary Colors

This is just like it sounds. It is created by drawing a square shape in the color wheel and using the opposing four colors indicated. This color scheme can be useful if done well, but if not it can be catastrophic. Choosing one of these four colors to dominate a design while the others "support" that color is often the best option.

SQUARE COMPLEMENTARY

Triadic Color Schemes

These color schemes are created by choosing a set of three colors on the wheel that are equidistant from each other. The primary colors, for example, are a triadic color scheme. Some other triadic color schemes are shown below. By using a triadic color scheme you naturally create contrast, but the colors must be used thoughtfully to create balance.

TRIADIC COLOR SCHEMES

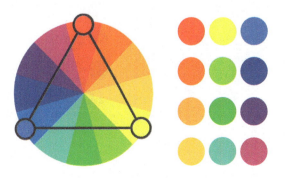

Analogous Color Schemes

Choosing a combination of three to five adjacent color hues on the wheel creates what is called an analogous color scheme. Since these colors are more closely related, you have to be more strategic to achieve contrast. By using one dominant color and one to two of the other colors to support it, as well as one to two more of the colors to accent your design, you should have the best chance of a successful color combination.

ANALOGOUS COLOR SCHEMES

Monochromatic Color Scheme

Mono means one, so this should help give a hint about what this color scheme is based on. By using one color and utilizing that color's tints, shades, and tones, you can create an interesting visual in a monochromatic color scheme.

MONOCHROMATIC COLOR SCHEMES

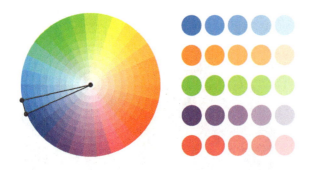

Choosing Your Color Scheme

When choosing your project's color scheme, consider what mood and emotions you are trying to evoke. Although there are established color recommendations and rules to follow, be creative and experiment to find the right balance of contrast and cohesion for your specific brand or project. There are endless online resources to look to for color scheme inspiration, which is where I like to start. It can also be a good option to look to the natural world to find a color scheme — from flowers to oceans to deserts.

RGB Color Mode & Hex Color Codes

This should be familiar from the common terms list at the beginning of this book. As I mentioned, RGB is used for digital display such as anything online, television, electronics etc. It uses red, green and blue light to create all the other colors. What is most important to remember is to choose RGB color formatting when working on a digital project.

The hex color system converts each RGB number value to a hexadecimal representation giving you a six character code that can be used in most design programs to specify a consistent color.

For example:

38   Graphic Design Fundamentals • An Introduction & Workbook for Beginners

CMYK Color Mode

This is the color combination used in print media. CMYK stands for cyan, magenta, yellow, and key, or black, ink colors that combine to create the whole variety of print colors available. When working on a print project, be sure to set your file to CMYK mode, so that what you see on screen will most closely represent what the printed out version will look like.

You have a very short window of time to grab a viewer's attention, and color is a super effective way to accomplish this if you use it effectively. Don't forget to create contrast. Draw the viewer's eye but don't overwhelm them, which can lead to confusion and cause them to keep scrolling.

Here are some tried and true color tips from referenced sources.

Murch, G. M., in his book; *The Effective Use of Color* (1983), makes these recommendations:

- Avoid pure blue for text.
- Avoid thin lines and small shapes.
- Avoid red and green in the periphery of large-scale displays.
- Note that all colors are equally discernible.
- Do not overuse color.
- Use similar color to convey similar meaning.
- Use common background color for group-related elements.
- Use brightness and saturation to attract attention.
- Taking into account color-deficient viewers, avoid single color distinction.

Color combinations for user interfaces with graphic displays as recommended by Brown & Cunningham in 1989:

Background	Best colors	Worst colors
White	Black, Blue	Cyan, Yellow
Black	Yellow, White	Blue
Red	Black	Blue, Magenta
Green	Black, Red	Cyan
Blue	Red, White, Yellow	Black
Cyan	Blue, Red	Green, White, Yellow
Magenta	Black, Blue	Cyan, Green
Yellow	Black, Blue	Cyan, White

10 Questions to ask ABOUT COLOR

1 What does the color represent?

change • intelligence • meaning
prosperity • growth • health
practicality • empathy
productivity • idealism
calmness • balance
flexibility • discovery
acceptance • belief • faith
trust • understanding
wisdom • truth • dignity
creativity • originality

enlightenment • awareness
optimism • clarity
enthusiasim • satisfaction
warmth • excitement
friendship • confidence
influence • happiness
success • attraction
desire • determination
adventure • strength
love • power • energy

2 Once you pick a dominant color, try an analogous color scheme to see how that looks.

3 If that doesn't get your desired effect, then move on to more contrast with a complementary color scheme.

4 Does that feel like too much? Time to try and split the difference with a split complementary scheme.

Graphic Design Fundamentals • An Introduction & Workbook for Beginners

10 Questions to ask ABOUT COLOR

5. Or do you want more color options to bring more variety? Then move on to try square complementary.

6. Too much going on now? Pull it back a bit and try a triadic color scheme next.

7. Still not finding what you are looking for? Never underestimate a monochromatic approach and don't be afraid to give it a try.

8. Experiment with your tints, shades and tones and you can really create some visual interest with one dominant color.

9. Once you have your color scheme in mind, experiment with accent colors and variety to see if you want to turn it up or tone it down.

10. Know your ultimate project purpose so that you can build your design in the right color format right from the start. CMYK or RGB?*

*Or a more advanced option might be using Pantone colors, but that is a whole different book.

Graphic Design Fundamentals • An Introduction & Workbook for Beginners

Chapter Eight
TYPEFACE OR FONT?

The terms "typeface" and "font" are used interchangeably these days, but are they historically the same thing? No.

The term "font" is very widely used incorrectly, but it doesn't really matter anymore unless you are a graphic designer, and then it might be good to know.

A typeface is a set of glyphs (an alphabet, numbers and punctuation) that share a common design, considered a "font family". For example, Arial is a common typeface. A font is a set of glyphs WITHIN a typeface. This just means that while Arial is the typeface, 12 point Arial is a font, and 24 point Arial is a separate font, while 12 point bold Arial is yet another font.

As you can imagine, there are technically a ton of different fonts within one typeface. The reasons for understanding the difference between these two is not as important these days as it was in the era when text was set by a typesetter by hand before printing. Now you know the difference between the two and can properly use these terms in the design world.

Fonts are one of my very favorite things to discuss. I have created hundreds of font families from scratch and love finding new typefaces that inspire me.

Picking Pairings

Let's talk about picking typefaces for a project. There are so many font families that you can easily go down a rabbit hole and get lost trying to figure out what goes with what. With just a few basic principles you can narrow down your typeface search.

TYPEFACE
(OR FONT FAMILY)

Arial • **Arial Bold** • *Arial Italic*

Arial 18 point

and so on...

FONTS

1. Arial Regular 12 point
2. Arial Bold 16 point
3. Arial Italic 9 point

1. **Concordance** – this is when all the type on your design is similar, typically just one typeface with multiple fonts, possibly bold or larger versions. This is often the clear choice for layouts with lots of text like books or more formal documents.
2. **Contrasting** – this is achieved when you use two or more typefaces that are obviously different but work well together.
3. **Conflicting** – this is when two typefaces are too similar and cause visual confusion.

A graphic designer's main goal is usually to try to achieve concordance or contrasting type but avoid conflicting type. Let's talk about how to work towards achieving the desired effect with type.

Concordance

This is the simplest way to pick a variety of fonts since they are all in the same family. By utilizing the italic, bold, and size style options for a typeface, you can create a cohesive appearance while also offering visual contrast, even if it tends to be more minimal. This option works best with typefaces that offer a larger variety of style choices, sometimes called a font superfamily. These superfamilies ideally have serif and sans-serif options, but since they are designed in the same font family they should share characteristics that keep them related and working well together. By using different sizes, weight, capitals, and so on, you can easily pair fonts from the same family to create a clean organized design.

Contrasting

While often considered a more difficult method to pair fonts, contrasting is also thought to create more unique and visually successful layouts. I find that experimentation is the best way to see what typefaces can work well together, but there are some more concrete attributes to consider if you prefer that method. Finding two typefaces that are different enough to create contrast, but that share something in common such as weight, direction, character shape, character height, serif or sans-serif, and so on will usually help you create a successful pairing.

Using the font Rockwell from the serif category as a headline and subheader for consistency and then using the sans serif font Arboria for the body text, creates a nice visual contrast without being too confusing.

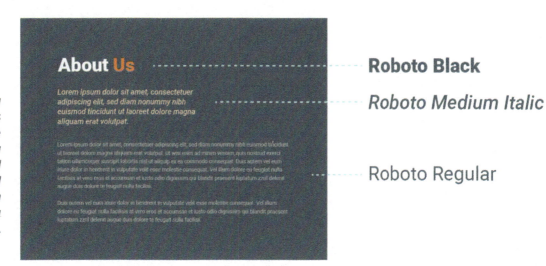

By just using different styles of the same Roboto font you can create visual hierarchy and contrast with an easy font pairing option.

Graphic Design Fundamentals • An Introduction & Workbook for Beginners

Conflicting

This can occur when you have not created enough contrast between two typefaces, resulting in an unappealing visual conflict instead of harmonious pairing.

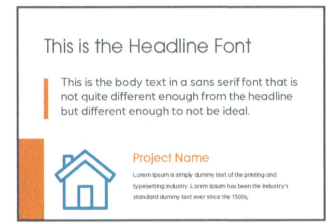

Using the sans serif font Avant Garde Gothic for the headline, and then using the sans serif font Arboria for the body text, is not enough of a contrast to create balance and just creates visual confusion.

Here are some helpful ways to avoid creating conflict in your typeface pairings.

1. Choose from different categories – serif, sans serif, script, and decorative.
2. Remember to incorporate the hierarchy principle of size to create type contrast.
3. Using the hierarchy principle of color is another great way to visually contrast two typefaces.
4. It is almost never a good idea to combine two script typefaces or two decorative typefaces, and should only be done with extreme confidence.

While rules and guidelines are important to learn and refer to, part of what I love about design is breaking the rules and going outside the box, so I don't want you to be afraid to do that! Just practice and play to gain more confidence in your type layout skills. A few rules I tend to try to follow are:

1. Never have more than three typefaces in one design. Typically, I only have two.
2. Once you choose a typeface for a project that is multiple pages, consistency is key! Keep the chosen formatting going throughout the design.
3. Know your medium. I design differently for a website versus a print project, and typeface choices are part of that.
4. Keep your typeface choice in the style of the theme of the project. For instance, don't use a spooky typeface for a corporate brochure or a professional looking typeface for a toy store.

The Four Types of Typefaces

Most typefaces fall into four broad categories: serif, sans serif, scripts, and decorative. However, within these groups are many subcategories. Let's start with the main two categories: serif and sans-serif.

This is considered the oldest font type and originated in Roman carvings. The serifs on the letters is thought to have been either deliberate by the carvers as decorative or inevitable as they created the outline of the letters. Whatever it was, these serif fonts became the first type of letters used in print. Because of this, serif typefaces are considered to bring feelings of tradition and history, but there are also more modern options in this family. Typically serif font families are broken down further into four categories: old style, transitional, modern, and square.

Old Style
This category of typefaces is thought to have originated around 1465 and is characterized by the curves that connect the serif to the stroke and minimal contrast between thick-and-thin lines. This style is rarely seen online, but is used in print, posters, logos, etc. Some examples include Garamond, Palatino, Bookerly, Cartier, Callisto, and Requiem.

Transitional
Typefaces in the transitional category can be traced back to the 18th century at a time of transition between old style and modern design. There is more contrast between thick and thin strokes than in old style typefaces, and serifs are thinner and flat as well as utilizing a more vertical axis. Some examples include Times New Roman, Baskerville, Georgia, Bookman and Cambria.

Modern (Neoclassical, Didone)
In the late 18th century, this more delicate style of serif fonts was created to show the more refined printing techniques available. Modern typefaces are characterized by a dramatic contrast between the thick and thin strokes and narrow serifs with a constant width. These serif typefaces are the most common serif on the web and are often used in fashion and furniture marketing. Some examples include Bodoni, Fenice, Didot, and Moderno.

Slab or Square
Typefaces belonging to this early 19th century style were created to draw attention, so they have very heavy square serifs and hardly any stroke contrast. They are often geometric or square in style, hence the name. Some examples include Rockwell, Soho, and Clarendon.

Sans Serif

These types of fonts appeared when minimalism became popular along with the desire to have cleaner, simpler typefaces. These typefaces are without, or "sans" serifs. These types of fonts are the most prevalent in today's culture. There are also four types of subcategories for sans serif typefaces.

Grotesque

This was the first popular sans serif typeface category. They got their name just because they were so different than any previously known typeface. Their distinguishing features include little contrast in stroke weight, a squared look to some curves, a standout capital "R", and irregular proportions. These types of fonts are still being created today and can be quite unique. Some examples include Eurostile, News Gothic, and Franklin Gothic.

Neo-Grotesque

You might have guessed from the name that these font families are a more modern version of the grotesque typefaces. These fonts were created in the 1950s and are a thinner, plainer version of a sans serif typeface. Helvetica was created during this time and is still very prevalent today, as well as Arial and Impact.

Geometric

These typefaces are based on simple geometric shapes such as squares and circles. They became popular because they looked even cleaner and more modern than the neo-grotesque font families. The letter "o" is almost a perfect circle, and the capital letters are all different widths. The first geometric typeface is called Erbar. Other popular examples are Gotham and Century Gothic.

Humanistic

This type style was supposed to look more hand drawn, hence the name. They are a combination of sans serif typefaces with the more traditional serif look intended to increase readability. They are based on the proportions of Roman capitals and old style lowercase, with little visual stroke contrast, as well as a calligraphic influence. Some examples include Gill Sans, Myriad, and Calibri.

Graphic Design Fundamentals • An Introduction & Workbook for Beginners

Script typefaces are intended to resemble handwriting and are often cursive in nature and intricate in design. For these reasons they are not often used online or in marketing where legibility is vital. They should never be used for body text and typically are seen in invitations, logos, packaging, posters, etc. There are five subcategories of script typefaces – formal, casual, calligraphic, blackletter, and handwriting.

Formal

Formal script typefaces are very elegant font families characterized by flowing loops and flourishes with graceful strokes that often have each letter connected to the next.

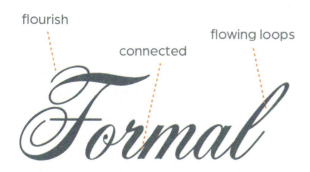

Casual

These scripts are designed to look informal, hand drawn, and relaxed. Their strokes can be connected or not.

Calligraphic

Calligraphic type styles often look as if they were drawn with flat-tipped pens or brushes and are intended to imitate the hand drawn work of a calligrapher. Their strokes can be connected or not as well.

appear to be drawn with a brush or pen

Calligraphic

Blackletter

These styles came from the early handwritten forms of religious texts. This style was used to set the first book printed with movable type – the Gutenberg Bible. They are characterized by a thick, black appearance, and intricate decorated caps with the lowercase characters being narrow with dramatic strokes.

intricate ornaments   thick, black appearance

Blackletter

Handwriting

These typefaces are just like they sound – intended to represent handwriting and can even be created directly from handwriting samples. These font families are vastly different and can be anything from a beautiful script to scratchy child-like lettering.

represent handwriting

Handwriting

This category covers a wide range of typefaces that don't really fit into any of the other categories. They are also sometimes referred to as display font families, as they are most often designed with that idea in mind. They are unique and diverse, and intended to grab attention with their thematic visual appeal. They really do not follow any rules or guidelines or really share any characteristics with other decorative typefaces. They should only be used for titles and never body text.

Principles of Typography Layout

As you might have guessed, fonts are my passion, and I believe that they are one of the most important part of any design. Three important terms to know when laying out your typefaces are leading, kerning, and tracking.

Leading

Leading determines how text is spaced vertically or how much space is between the different lines of text. This occurs every time your text goes over one line, so I am sure you have seen this already, but whether you have adjusted your leading is the question. Three things to keep in mind when determining the leading of your text block are the baseline, the descenders, and the ascenders. Your baseline is where the letters sit and the descenders are the characters or letters that sit below the baseline while the ascenders are those characters that are taller such as 'k' or a 't'.

A typical default leading is set to be about 20 percent larger than the font size. You can adjust the leading to create different text effects.

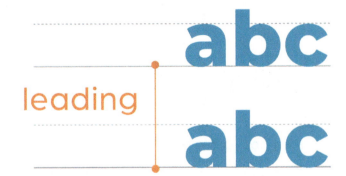

Kerning

Kerning is the distance between two letters. If the kerning is too short, words can become unreadable, but if you set the kerning too wide, then the text is equally hard to read. Adjusting the kerning is sometimes necessary to achieve the optical illusion that the characters are set equally apart, as the actual mathematical spacing might not look just right.

kerning

When I create fonts, I always look at the different kerning between each letter, as the different shapes of each letter make it an interesting puzzle to make fit. Letters such as a lowercase 'j' or uppercase 'T' require manual adjustment with other letters to achieve a balanced appearance.

Adjusting the kerning of your text might not be necessary most of the time, but especially with headlines and titles you will want to know how to adjust it and when it would improve the appearance.

Tracking

This is similar to kerning, but instead of adjusting the space between specific characters, it refers to adjusting the space between ALL of the characters in your text at one time. This is often done to create a modern, simple effect to a word or line of text in a headline or logo. It shouldn't really be adjusted too much in bodies of text, as it can quickly ruin the legibility of your text.

tracking

Where to Find Fonts?

There are a ton of free fonts online that you can use for personal projects. It is important to note that you should read and understand the licenses provided with fonts in regard to how they can be used legally. If you intend to use a font in a commercial project, you should have purchased the proper license that allows such usage.

A quick online search will show you the latest websites where you can download free fonts or paid fonts, and even better font bundles! Installation of font files is easier than it sounds. I recommend an online search of your specific system – Mac, Windows, etc. – and you will be inundated with how-to videos and tutorials. Installing a font should take less than a minute. I could go on and on for days about typefaces and designing fonts, but that definitely feels like another book, so let's put that aside for now and continue on our way!

7 Typographic CONTRASTS

Here are the seven typographic contrasts as outlined by the godfather of modern typography, Canadian typographer Carl Dair, one of the greatest 20th-century designers. His main idea is one I believe strongly in which is that text is never just incidental in graphic design. It's an art.

SIZE
You will see this everywhere in graphic design and is the most obvious way to create contrast in type. Placing large text next to small text will draw the viewer's eye immediately and create visual contrast.

WEIGHT
By using different line widths, such as bold styles, you can make it stand out.

FORM
This refers to the basic shapes of characters of a typeface. Uppercase and lowercase are naturally contrasting versions of a typeface form.

STRUCTURE
The shape of each letter as it fits into the typeface as a whole. The most common way to create structural contrast is to use two different typefaces from two different categories.

TEXTURE
This is the combination of form and structure, defined by Dair as the aesthetic of the text as a whole. Rather than looking at each character individually, this considers the text as a whole line or block, how it fits and interacts with other lines or blocks, and how they contrast to each other.

DIRECTION
Just like it sounds, this involves the horizontal or vertical layout of text and all the angles in between. Turning a word even to a slight angle creates a visual contrast. Turning a whole block of text on its side can create a more impactful contrast.

COLOR
We have already learned how important color is to creating hierarchy and contrast, as well as visual balance, so it should come as no surprise that it matters what color your text is. Dair reminds us that nothing is more contrasting than black text on a white background or vice versa.

Graphic Design Fundamentals • An Introduction & Workbook for Beginners

Chapter Nine
WHAT PROGRAM TO USE?

Adobe (Illustrator, Photoshop & InDesign)

You probably already know about this robust graphic software company and at least some of their numerous graphic programs. This is what I use for all of my design projects. Adobe is largely considered the industry standard and is often even required when working with companies or printers in order to be able to create the formats that they need.

Adobe Illustrator

Illustrator is a vector based software, so you can literally create designs that can be used at any size. This makes Illustrator very versatile, and it can be used to create anything ranging from logos, illustrations, web designs, graphics, icons, and even text documents. Remember what you know about vector versus raster images, meaning you can basically resize designs to any size in Illustrator without losing quality, as opposed to images in Photoshop, which can become grainy or blurry if made too large.

Use Illustrator for creating:

- logos
- illustrations
- graphics
- documents with images and text, but it is not ideal for multi-page documents

Adobe Photoshop

Photoshop is a raster based software and although it is a powerful tool, it is important to remember that images cannot be resized larger without losing quality. Photoshop is perfect for editing photos, but not necessarily for layouts that have text included. It can be limiting if used for designing layouts for print or web.

Photoshop is ideal for editing and creating photos, creating banner ads, editing pictures for print, and designing video graphics. On the other hand, Photoshop is not the right program for creating logos, because you won't be able to manipulate or enlarge your files the way you can with a file from Illustrator.

Photoshop is ideal for editing photos but can also be used for:

- creating banner ads that have photos in them
- creating icons and images for the web, if you prefer it over Illustrator

Adobe InDesign

InDesign is intended for laying out printed materials and is frequently used for book interiors. It's also ideal for annual reports, newsletters, brochures, or anything that would benefit from master page layouts and includes multiple pages. InDesign was created to work seamlessly with Photoshop and Illustrator, and to allow users to take elements from both and put them together in a single document.

Like Illustrator, InDesign is a vector based program with the primary difference being the focus on the master and multiple page aspects. Although some people like to do layouts of multiple pages in Illustrator it really is not ideal for books or multiple page projects. Layouts created in Illustrator tend to be unnecessarily large files and cause issues in the commercial printer world. Packaged InDesign files that include all of the 'linked' images are ideal for printers.

Use InDesign for:

- creating a book layout
- creating newsletters, brochures, or anything that has master pages and multiple pages
- PDF documents

Canva

This online application has allowed many people to tap into their inner designer with easily editable templates and drag and drop functionality. It has a free option that you can experiment with before deciding if you need a paying option. It includes stock photos and icons that make designing social media graphics a quick and easy project. It has limitations for extensive graphic projects and can be frustrating to seasoned graphic designers, but is a great option for beginners or non-designers who have a good visual eye.

GIMP

This historically free software is an acronym for GNU Image Manipulation Program. It can be used as a simple paint program, a photo editing program, an online batch processing system, a mass production image renderer, an image format converter, and more.

It is designed to be augmented with plug-ins and extensions to do just about anything. The advanced scripting interface allows everything from the simplest task to the most complex image manipulation procedures to be easily scripted for those who are familiar with how to do that.

It is considered similar to Photoshop and can be a good option for those starting out before making a larger investment in the Adobe Suite.

Inkspace

Inkscape is a free and open source vector graphics editor for GNU/Linux, Windows and MacOS X. It is similar to Illustrator in capability and has features for both artistic and technical illustration. Inkscape uses the standardized SVG file format as its main format, which is supported by many other applications, including web browsers.

PowerPoint

Many novice designers have used PowerPoint at some point to create something other than what it was intended for. PowerPoint is intended to be used to create presentations, and that is truly all it is really capable of. You will undoubtedly run into issues if you try to use PowerPoint for print projects, logo design, graphic design, and so on. If this is the software you are comfortable with, then I would just advise you to work towards learning a new, more powerful design program.

Make the Choice

Ultimately, choosing a design software has a lot of factors to consider, not the least of which is cost, but with subscriptions and such, many of them are more affordable than ever. I would only advise not to be afraid of learning something new and let that keep you from expanding your graphic design software knowledge. Just jump in!

Conclusion

You made it! In the following pages you will discover some helpful resources and tools to help you on your graphic design journey.

Don't forget to check out my additional books to extend your graphic design progress even more. I can't wait to see your designs online so feel free to tag @ktdesignacademy.

Follow me on Amazon to hear about my latest book releases and don't forget to leave a review, as it is essential to all authors!

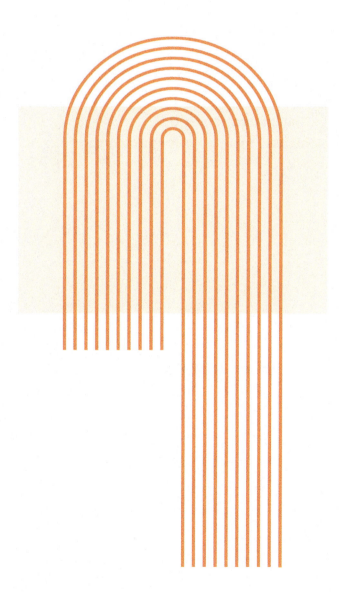

BONUS ONE

DESIGN *Inspiration* RESOURCES

Below are some **inspiration** destinations you can check out to get started.

Pinterest (obvious one, but always good!)
www.pinterest.com

Notes:

The Inspiration Grid
https://theinspirationgrid.com

Notes:

Type Hunting (typography inspiration)
https://typehunting.com/

Notes:

Graphic Design Fundamentals • An Introduction & Workbook for Beginners

DESIGN INSPIRATION
Resources

Logo Joy (database of popular logo designs)
https://looka.com/logo-ideas/

Notes:

Logo Pond (logo inspiration)
https://logopond.com/

Notes:

Logo of the Day (logo ideas)
https://logooftheday.com/

Notes:

DESIGN INSPIRATION
Resources

Type Goodness (typography inspiration)
http://typegoodness.com/

Notes:

Behance (Adobe's designer showcase)
https://www.behance.net/

Notes:

Masterpicks (graphic design inspiration)
https://www.themasterpicks.com/

Notes:

DESIGN INSPIRATION
Resources

Type Everything (typography inspiration)
https://typeverything.com/

Notes:

Wix (creative design blog)
https://www.wix.com/blog/creative

Notes:

Fonts in Use (collection of font examples)
https://fontsinuse.com/blog

Notes:

DESIGN INSPIRATION
Resources

DIELINE (packaging inspiration)
https://thedieline.com/

Notes:

Identity Designed (identify inspiration)
https://identitydesigned.com/

Notes:

Mindsparkle Magazine (daily design inspiration)
https://mindsparklemag.com/

Notes:

DESIGN INSPIRATION
Resources

Name:

Link:

Notes:

Name:

Link:

Notes:

Name:

Link:

Notes:

BONUS TWO

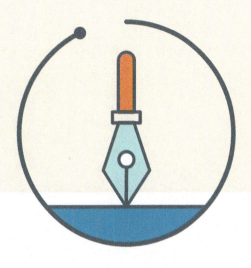

GETTING
Started

[WORKBOOK]

Graphic Design Fundamentals • An Introduction & Workbook for Beginners

PROJECT NAME

Describe the company **brand**.

Describe the **target** audience.

Does the company have a specific **color** palette?

Are there specific **fonts, icons, or images** associated with the company?

Any **restrictions or limitations** to consider?

NEXT STEP
Brainstorm

WORDS

List any words that you can think of associated with the company brand.

INSPIRATION

Use these words to help find visual inspiration for your project. Use google images, Pinterest, or any of the other inspiration resources supplied in your **Inspiration Resource Guide**.

PROCESS OPTIONS

Create a subfolder in your project folder or drive to save your inspiration images.

Create a secret Pinterest board and name it for your project.

Pin or save images that you find any inspiration in, no matter how small.

Save the images with a note to your self to help you remember what inspired you.

Search using the words you came up with as well as the type of project.

Search using the company color palette to find complementary colors.

Review your pins and saved images and delete any to narrow down your ideas.

Decide what you are **ready** to do next:

MORE THINKING

START SKETCHING

BEGIN A DESIGN

Graphic Design Fundamentals • An Introduction & Workbook for Beginners

OTHER BRAINSTORM IDEAS

Examine your saved/pinned images and decide what parts you are most inspired by – make a note of them here. (for example, the curve of a line, the shape of an image, the shade of a color, etc.)

List the colors that you are definitely wanting to include and maybe those you definitely don't want to include.

Summarize your creative aesthetic ideas as much as you can as succinctly as you can to focus your ideas and your creativity in one direction.

OPTIONS Sketch

GRAB YOUR PENCIL

Use these thumbnails to start sketching your ideas no matter how rough. Or grab a blank journal to organize your sketches and ideas. Whatever works for you!

Sketch title/notes:

Sketch title/notes:

Sketch title/notes:

Sketch title/notes:

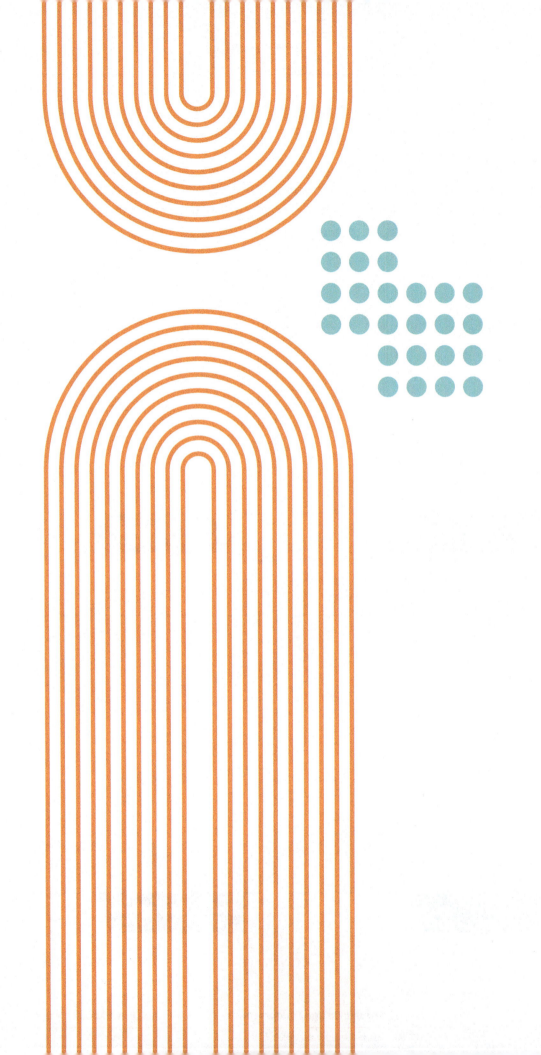

BONUS THREE

ADOBE
Illustrator

GUIDE

MEET ADOBE Illustrator

1 **The Menu Bar:** Includes the File, Edit, and other menus that give you access to a variety of commands, adjustments, settings, and panels.

2 **Tools Panel:** Contains the tools for creating and editing artwork. You can customize the tools that display here and there are additional tools that display in the ones with the white corner triangle that you can access by holding down the mouse over that tool.

3 **Panels:** These contain different controls to edit your artwork including Properties, Layers, and Artboards. You can customize displays with what is most helpful to your current project.

4 **Document Window:** Displays the file you're currently working on.

Tool Panel & Shortcuts

ADOBE Illustrator

Common Shortcuts

Function	MAC	Windows
Create a new document	Command + N	Ctrl + N
Open a document	Command + O	Ctrl + O
Save a document	Command + S	Ctrl + S
View at 100%	Command + 1	Ctrl +1
Fit to screen	Command + 0	Ctrl + 0
Zoom in	Command + (+)	Ctrl + (+)
Zoom out	Command + (–)	Ctrl + (–)
Duplicate an object	Option + drag	Alt + drag
Revert a doc to original	F12	F12
Toggle screen modes	F	F
Default fill/stroke colors	D	D
Toggle fill/stroke	X	X
Lock selection	Command + 2	Ctrl + 2
Lock all artwork	Command + Shift + Option + 2	Ctrl + Shift + Alt + 2
Unlock all artwork	Command + Option + 2	Ctrl + Alt + 2
Align paragraph(s) center	Command + Shift + C	Ctrl + Shift + C
Align paragraph(s) left	Command + Shift + L	Ctrl + Shift + L
Align paragraph(s) right	Command + Shift + R	Ctrl + Shift + R
Justify paragraph(s)	Command + Shift + J	Ctrl + Shift + J
Insert soft return	Shift + Enter	Shift + Enter

ADOBE Illustrator

Useful File Formats

AI
Adobe Illustrator's standard vector file format.
Useful to always keep a source file in this format for any project.

EPS
EPS is a PostScript image file format.
Since it is compatible with other graphics applications, it can be used to transfer files to individuals who may not be using Illustrator.

SVG
Scalable Vector Graphics (SVG)
An XML-based vector image format for 2D graphics. It is also compatible with graphics applications other than Illustrator, so it is often used for file transfers.

PDF
Adobe's Portable Document Format.
Unlike other PDFs, this particular format preserves all the data in the original file. Ideal whenever you're trying to open artwork in different Creative Cloud apps.

ADOBE Illustrator

Useful Features

Pathfinder
These tools allow you to combine objects into new shapes with options like Unite, Divide, and Trim.

Brushes
You can change the appearance of a path with a brush. There are different types of brushes to achieve different effects: calligraphic, scatter, art, pattern, and bristle.

Convert Text to Outlines
You can convert any text (typed using a font) into vector artwork. Create outlines of any text, but once you do this you cannot edit the text, and can only edit the now vector shaped letters.
Shortcut: select the text and shift + command + O

Image Trace
Use this tool to turn an existing piece of artwork (like a raster image or a drawing you made) into a vector object. Choose from different modes like B&W, line art, or color, and tweak the different options to create varying levels of detail.

ADOBE Illustrator

The Pen Tools

How to Use the Pen Tool to Create Lines

Pen Tool – Straight Lines
Select the Pen Tool, click to create points, and they'll connect to form straight lines. You can add a point to close these lines, forming a closed shape.

Create Curved Lines
While you are creating individual points with the Pen Tool, you can click and drag any one of those points to add what is called Bezier handles. These can be dragged to change the curve.

Delete Anchor Point Tool
Hover over any point you've created and simply click to delete it.

Add Anchor Point Tool
Hover over a section of a line, and the cursor will display the option to add a new point.

Anchor Point Tool
Hover over any anchor point for the option to select and alter it.

ADOBE
Illustrator

The Selection Tools

Different Options for Manipulating an Object

Selection Tool (V)
Click on any object, line, or shape to select it.

Direct Selection Tool (A)
Use this to move individual points in your shapes or line segments.
Shortcut: hold down COMMAND/CTRL while using the default Selection tool.

Move Bezier Handles
With the same Direct Selection tool, you can adjust Bezier handles to change curves.

Turn a Straight Line into a Curved Line
Use the Anchor Point tool to click and hold the point you want to change until handles appear, creating a curved (Bezier) line.

Shortcut: hold OPTION/ALT while using the Pen Tool.

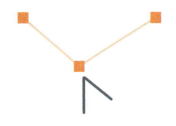

Turning Curves into Straight Lines
You can use the same Anchor Point tool to remove handles and turn your curve into a straight line.

ADOBE Illustrator

The Type Tools

Use these tools to add text to your document.

Type Tool (T)
Use this tool to click and add text to any document. Drag the tool to create a text container.

Vertical Type Tool
This tool allows you to type your text vertically instead of horizontally.

Area Type Tool
This allows you to convert an existing shape into a text box and type in it.

Vertical Area Type Tool
Just like the area type tool, but it allows you to type vertically instead of horizontally.

Type on a Path Tool
This tool allows you to use an existing line or shape as a path to type on. Simply click on the path to add editable text.

Vertical Type on a Path Tool
Just like the type on a path tool, but it allows you to type vertically instead of horizontally.

Touch Type Tool
This allows you to select individual letters of existing text and move them around.

ADOBE Illustrator

Other Tools

Curvature Tool (shift+)
The curvature tool is an awesome way to create vector shapes, especially those with curved edges.

Mesh Tool (U)
This tool allows you to select certain points within a specific section of your shape to add another color, allowing the colors to combine into a gradient effect, acting as highlights, shading, and natural color progression.

Gradient Tool (G)
This tool creates either linear or radial gradients within a shape or line.

Blend Tool (W)
This tool allows you to take two different colored objects and create a gradient blend between them.

Artboard Tool (shift+O)
Use this tool to add a new artboard or resize your current artboards.

Zoom Tool (Z)
The zoom tool zooms in and out of your workspace.

JUMP IN!
Start Designing!

Creating a New Illustrator Document

Open Adobe Illustrator.

1 When you open Illustrator, you'll see the Start workspace. Click **Create new** to open the New Document dialog box, or simply press Control+N (Windows) or Command+N, (macOS) or you can simply click on one of the **presets** provided at the top.

2 Select a category at the top such as Print, Mobile, or Web. These presets will prove very helpful in suggesting color modes, sizes, resolution, etc.

Tip: Decide on your project before choosing a category. Choose Print if you're designing a flyer, business card, or logo; choose Web if you plan to work on a web banner, social graphic, or art for your blog. If you're unsure of the final destination, select Art & Illustration and customize the settings for your project.

Graphic Design Fundamentals • An Introduction & Workbook for Beginners

NEW DOCUMENT

3 Once you select a category, you'll see presets for commonly used document types. This can be a great starting point to create a blank document using predefined dimensions and settings. For example, after picking Print, you can select a letter size file.

4 You can customize your document on the right side, whether or not you picked a preset. In the panel on the right, you can specify exact dimensions, alter measurement units, page orientation, add a print bleed, etc.

5 When you're ready, click **Create** This will open a new document with a blank artboard all set up and ready for you.

You can change the settings at any point. Details on how to change them can be found on the next pages.

ILLUSTRATOR
Tips

Edit an artboard

An artboard is like your canvas for your creations. Artboards can be of any size and your document can actually contain numerous artboards which can also be different sizes, so you can easily design for different projects and output sizes all at once.

If your **Properties** panel is not visible, go to the Window menu and select **Properties**. With nothing selected in your document, click **Edit Artboards** (as shown).

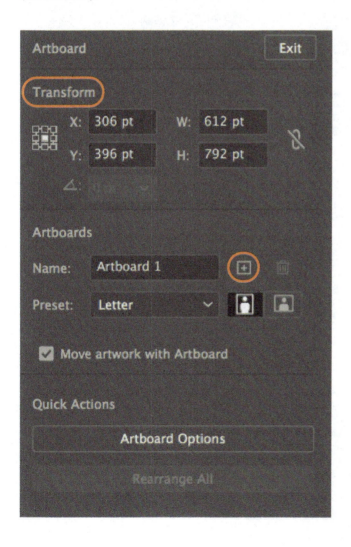

You can edit the width and height of the artboard by typing new values in the boxes under Transform. Click the New Artboard icon (highlighted) to create additional artboards. You can select a preset from the drop down. Click an artboard to select it and you can manually adjust it by dragging the edges, or delete it by pressing the delete key.

When you're done making edits, press Esc or click the Exit button at the top of the Properties panel.

Graphic Design Fundamentals • An Introduction & Workbook for Beginners

Edit the document

It is easy to make a change to your entire document consisting of numerous artboards. In the **Properties** panel, click **Document Setup** under **Quick Actions**. Change the units or bleed settings, and then click OK.

Another option is to click **Preferences** in the **Properties** panel to access and edit any of the Illustrator application settings to your preference. (These preferences are saved when you quit Illustrator.)

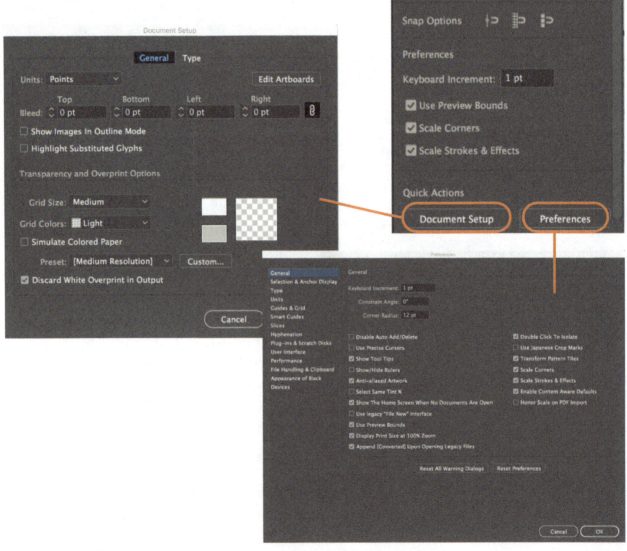

80 *Graphic Design Fundamentals* • An Introduction & Workbook for Beginners

ADOBE Illustrator

Expanded Tools

Note the shortcut keyboard letters next to each tool – these are essential to learn for the most common tools.

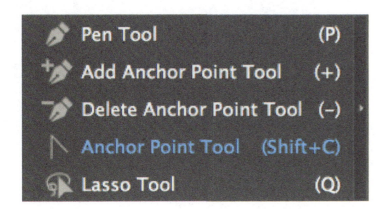

These tools are explained further on the Pen Tools page.

Lasso Tool (Q)
This works like the Direct Selection Tool, allowing you to select individual anchor points within a shape or object, but it works by drawing a shape around the points you want selected, making it a breeze to select multiple points at one time.

These tools are for adding text to your document.

These tools are explained in further detail on the Text Tools page.

Graphic Design Fundamentals • An Introduction & Workbook for Beginners

Expanded Tools

Direct Selection Tool (A)
The direct selection tool allows you to individually select and edit specific anchor points of vector shapes or lines.

Group Selection Tool
This tool allows you to easily select a specific object within a group in order to move, edit, or resize it individually.

Scale Tool (S)
This tool scales objects up using the center point as a marker. Hold down shift to constrain your proportions.

Shear Tool
This tool skews your objects at an angle. Hold down shift to constrain proportions.

Reshape Tool
This tool allows you to select multiple anchor points on a line or shape and move them all in one direction.

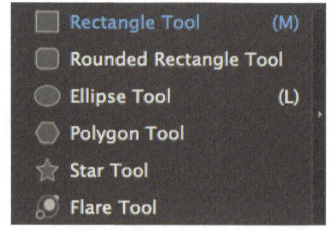

Rectangle Tool (M)
Used to create squares and rectangles.

Rounded Rectangle Tool
The same as the rectangle tool but with rounded corners.

Ellipse Tool (L)
Circles and ovals are created with this.

Polygon Tool
Use this to create any polygon from triangles to octagons and so on.

Star Tool
This makes stars! You can adjust the number of points on the star and how far the inner points go in.

Flare Tool
Not often used, this tool does just what it says: it creates a flare shape.

Graphic Design Fundamentals • An Introduction & Workbook for Beginners

Expanded Tools

Rotate Tool (R)
This tool allows you to rotate shapes.

Reflect Tool (O)
This tool rotates an object as well but in a reflected state. Hold down shift to reflect it horizontally.

Line Segment Tool (\)
This tool creates individual lines. Hold down shift to keep them at 45 degree angles.

Arc Tool
Another way to create a arc or segment of an oval/circle.

Spiral Tool
Creates a spiral if you ever find yourself needing a spiral!

Rectangular Grid Tool
This tool is super handy to create a table that you can then edit the elements using the anchor points as well as change colors, line weights, etc.

Polar Grid Tool
This tool creates a round grid – kind of like a burner on a stove – if you find yourself needing such a thing.

Magic Wand Tool (Y)
Use this tool to click on a single object, and then automatically select everything else in your workspace with that same color.

Selection Tool (V)
This is the main selection tool, and you will find yourself using the shortcut (V) very often!

Expanded Tools

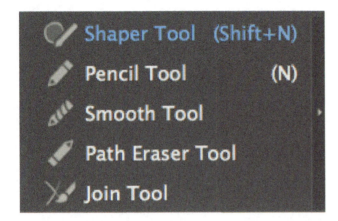

Shaper Tool (Shift+N)
This handy tool transforms your general shape into a cleaned up solid version. Try it!

Pencil Tool (N)
This acts similarly to the Paintbrush tool allowing freehand drawing.

Smooth Tool
This tool does just what it says and smooths out lines.

Path Eraser Tool
This allows you to erase part of a line.

Join Tool
This allows you to take two individual paths and merge them into one single path. Just select both paths and then use this tool to join them.

Paintbrush Tool (B)
Another letter you will find yourself typing a lot is the shortcut (B) to access this handy paintbrush tool.

Blob Brush Tool (Shift+B)
This is like the paintbrush tool but it creates a vector shape around the brushstroke creating an area instead of a path.

Eyedropper Tool (I)
This tool allows you to sample colors from shapes, lines, objects, or images so you can use that same color in other parts of your design.

Measure Tool
This tool allows you to click and drag between two points to measure the distance.

ADOBE Illustrator

Expanded Tools

Puppet Warp Tool
The Puppet Warp tool lets you twist and distort parts of your artwork. With it, you can add, move, and rotate pins to seamlessly transform your artwork into different variations.

Free Transform Tool (E)
This allows you to resize a shape in multiple ways.

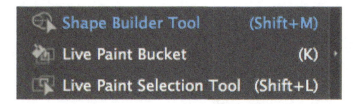

Shape Builder Tool (Shift+M)
This allows you to combine multiple, overlapping shapes into one.

Live Paint Bucket (K)
This allows you to easily fill shapes with colors or patterns.

Live Paint Selection Tool (Shift+L)
This allows you to select individual segments for your live paint area and adjust them.

Eraser Tool (Shift+E)
Wait for it – this erases! It can be very useful in editing out a portion of an object or path.

Scissors Tool (C)
Use this tool to cut a vector path or object.

Knife
This works like the scissors tool but has more freedom in how it cuts.

Hand Tool (H)
This is one of my favorite tools, and I type the letter H constantly. This allows you to move the view you have of your workspace.

Print Tiling Tool
This tool allows you to set up a printed item larger than a typical print area and accurately adjust how it will print on several pages.

ADOBE Illustrator

Expanded Tools

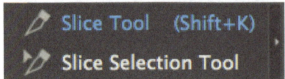

Width Tool (Shift+W)
This allows you to click on an area of a line and make the line stroke thicker or thinner.

Warp Tool (Shift+R)
This allows you to create warp effects on shapes and paths.

Twirl Tool
This distorts shapes by creating a twirl within them.

Pucker Tool
This puckers a shape creating a strong divot in them.

Bloat Tool
This bloats the selected shape, creating a bubble effect.

Scallop Tool
This works on shapes and lines and creates indents and bumps.

Crystallize Tool
This tool acts similarly to the scallop tool, but with larger indents and bumps.

Wrinkle Tool
This makes your shape or path wrinkled, adding bumps and wrinkles.

Slice Tool (Shift+K)
This allows you to separate your artboard into sections to save or export individually.

Slice Selection Tool
This allows you to select, change, move, and edit the slices you have made using the slice tool.

Expanded Tools

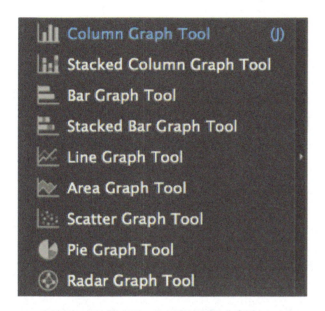

Column Graph Tool (J)
The column graph tool pops up a spreadsheet to input values to create a common column graph, which corresponds to values of the y-axis.

Stacked Column Graph Tool
This graph looks similar to the column graph, but the columns are segmented within itself, representing additional data from the chart.

Bar Graph Tool
A bar graph is a column graph facing horizontally instead of vertically, with the values of the bars aligning with the x-axis instead of the y-axis.

Stacked Bar Graph Tool
This bar graph includes segmented versions of each individual bar, to indicate more data than a typical bar graph does.

Line Graph Tool
A line graph uses points on the graph which are connected by a line.

Area Graph Tool
An area graph is similar in structure to a line graph but instead has shaded areas to include broader values of information.

Scatter Graph Tool
A scatter graph is made up of several points, scattered across the graph.

Pie Graph Tool
A classic pie chart where a circle is divided up into sections adding up to 100%.

Radar Graph Tool
A radar graph is similar to an area graph, but instead is round and can, therefore, have more variables than just two or four.

ADOBE Illustrator

Expanded Tools

Symbol Stainer Tool
This tool allows you to recolor individual symbols.

Symbol Screener Tool
This tool changes the opacity of individual symbols, making them lighter and lighter each time you click on them.

Symbol Styler Tool
This tool allows you to style your symbols more specifically by first using the Graphic Styles panel.

Symbol Sprayer Tool (Shift+S)
Open the symbol panel to select what symbol you want to be sprayed, then click and drag the spray can around your artboard to spray.

Symbol Shifter Tool
This tool allows you to move around symbols that have already been sprayed.

Symbol Scruncher Tool
This tool scrunches the symbols in towards the center.

Symbol Sizer Tool
This tool allows you to resize individual symbols after they have already been sprayed.

Symbol Spinner Tool
This allows you to rotate individual or multiple symbols at once.

Perspective Grid Tool (Shift+P)
The perspective grid tool allows you to make your creations look 3D by giving them spatial awareness.

Perspective Selection Tool (Shift+V)
The perspective selection tool allows you to edit and change around the perspective grid that appears on your artboard. Select the three points that appear on the bottom of the grid, and slide them around accordingly.

ADOBE
Illustrator

TIPS

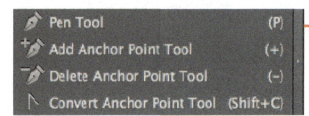

Click on this gray vertical bar to release these tools like below.

Click on these three dots at the bottom of the toolbar to open the editing toolbar area seen here.

Graphic Design Fundamentals • An Introduction & Workbook for Beginners

ABOUT THE AUTHOR

Kris Taft Miller

Kris joined Walt Disney Feature Animation directly out of college and spent eight years there, the first three in the Orlando studio and the remaining four in Los Angeles. She held numerous different types of roles in the Walt Disney Animation Communications department including graphic designer, art director, producer, writer, presenter, and editor. Her film credits include *Lilo & Stitch, Treasure Planet, Brother Bear, Home on the Range, Chicken Little,* and *Meet the Robinsons.*

She moved to North Carolina in 2004 to be with her husband, Jeremy. She started her own graphic design company, KT Design, LLC, and continues to freelance for Disney, as well as a large variety of other clients around the world. Her specialties include book covers and layouts, e-learning, logos, web design, and countless print projects.

She also runs a successful educational materials line for elementary school teachers under her Print Designs by Kris.com label. She lives in North Carolina with her husband and two sons. Working on her own book projects, as well as her two son's book projects, is one of her very favorite things to do!

LET'S CONNECT.

Website: ktdesignacademy.com

Join the Facebook Community: @ktdesignacademy

Tag me with your design creations so I can see your design progress!
#ktdesignacademy

Made in the USA
Coppell, TX
17 February 2025

46039652R00050